FIGHTING FOR JUSTICE FOR ALL

4-22-02

Thank michele
God bless you and Bless you
Herbert Andrew

An autobiography
by
Morris Hubert Andrew

Published and Distributed by:
Milligan Books, Inc.
An imprint of Professional Business Consultants
1425 W. Manchester Ave., Suite C
Los Angeles, California 90047
(323) 750-3592

Cover Design By
Chris Ebuehi – Graphic Options

Formatting By
Alpha Desktop Publishing

First Printing, March 2002
0987654321

Dedication

To my late darling wife. She was my editor. I had to rewrite my book many times before she said o.k. If I had not purchased my writing tablets from the 99 Cent Store; I would have been bankrupt (Smile)

During my earlier writing endeavor, she was my editor. I would never send out any correspondence without her stamp of Approval.

To my Mother who made her transition in Nov, 2000. She would have been 103 years of age on her birthday which was in December.

To all my grandchildren, great-grandchildren and neighbors' children who fondly call me "poppy"

To my beautiful children, I love you.

Table Of Contents

Preface

I've spent most of my life fighting for justice, not for myself, but for all—regardless of race, creed and color. Throughout the journey of my life, you will observe my fight to render justice wherever I witnessed injustice.

My editor asked me the following questions: Who influenced you to become such a fighter, and what are some of the occurrences or events that influenced your tenacity? I then began to realize that whether we are passive or assertive, someone has influenced our behavior.

As I look back on my childhood, I recall my father being very passive and my mother being extremely assertive and aggressive. My father showed extreme aggression when any of the children disobeyed our mother; after that he retreated back to his passive self. My mother responded in the same manner as my father when she felt that any of the children were disrespecting daddy.

There was never a question regarding the unity and respect between our parents. My mother was a fighter, she never compromised where injustice was an issue. Needless to say, I got my spirit and fight from her. My mother had the reputation of being a relentless fighter. In our little town, the people referred to her as the "Crazy Nigger," because mother as the old folks would say, didn't take wooden nickels for change.

I can recall several incidents that impacted my life.

In the south, white folk would refer to Blacks as Uncle and Aunt, rather calling them Mr. or Mrs. Most of the Whites called Black women girl and gal, and Black men they called boy. Whenever they referred to my mother as girl, she quickly responded, "I am not a girl, my name is Rudy."

My mother refused to go into any homes or businesses where Blacks were required to enter through the back door.

A house became available for sale in an all-white section of town. My mother initiated the purchase of that home, one half–block of land surrounded by whites. We were the only Blacks who lived in that section of town.

We never rode the public bus system until we came to California. People rode the bus from one small town to the next. Blacks had to sit in the back. My mother refused to ride public transportation. She walked until she was able to purchase a car.

After we moved to California, my mother went shopping in a retail store in the city of Southgate. The cashier and salespeople were looking at her with the, "why are you up in here attitude." My mother sensed their demeanor, and she began to give them a piece of her mind. They were startled, they changed their demeanor, and started apologizing to her.

My mother did not see skin color as a barrier; she taught us that justice was colorless. As I reflect back on my mother and these incidents, I know that I inherited my fight for justice for all from my mother.

INTRODUCTION

God has always made my life a beautiful one. I am Morris Hubert Andrew. I was born October 12, 1922, in Kaufmen, Texas. The town was so small that the trains did not whistle, let alone stop (smile). My parents are Bristol and Ruby Andrew. I have six brothers and one sister. My father, my mother and four of my brothers have expired. My mother's highest level of education was completion of high school. She worked from home doing sewing and clothes alterations. My mother encouraged her children to pursue higher learning. One of my brothers was a Dentist, one a Psychologist, one a Chiropractor, and one a School Administrator.

When I was growing up, children had a higher level of education than their parents. Today our youth do not seem to value education as much as the youth from yester years. It is not uncommon nowadays for the parents to have a higher level of education than their children. My mother made sure that all of us graduated from high school. What a role model!

My father had a very limited education, but he was a good provider. He worked in a retail store and did interior painting in homes. He would let me help him paint homes sometimes.

I can remember when the stock market crashed! All you could hear on the radio was about all the people that had lost all they had. They were jumping out of windows. It was a very sad time. The Depression set in. Jobs and money were very scarce. You had to do whatever work was available—from picking cotton to washing dishes. After picking cotton for a while, I decided it was not my "cup of tea." I was able to get a job washing dishes in a cafe. Later I became the Chef.

As far back as I can remember, my mother's greatest ambition was to leave Texas and move to Los Angeles, California. Her mother and her brother had moved to Los Angeles in the early 1920's. Her son, Chester, had moved to Los Angeles in the middle of the 1930's, and her son, Bristol, had moved later.

Then came the bombing of Pearl Harbor. We had not heard of Pearl Harbor before the bombing. The war was declared and men were being drafted for the Service. Jobs and money became more available.

My parents owned their own home. They bought a 1936 Ford sedan. Boy, were we styling!

Later, while my mother was visiting a neighbor, our home caught fire and was completely destroyed. We were very sad, and we were wondering what we were going to do. We stayed with some of my mother's friends. Then God stepped in and my brother, Bristol, sent us some money to help finance our moving to Los Angeles. We got ready in a hurry, and we were on our way to Los Angeles, California.

I drove all the way! We made lots of stops and enjoyed every mile of it. We had to sleep in the car and on the ground because Blacks could not stay in motels. After several days and nights we finally arrived in Los Angeles. We were very happy and pleased.

My brother Bristol allowed us to stay with him and his family until we could find and afford a place. My brother lived on Compton and Forty-first Place, very near Ross Snider Playground. We had lots of fun playing in the park. Compton Avenue and Forty-first Place was in close proximity to Central Avenue. That's when Central Avenue was really jumping. All the night clubs—The Memo, Club Alabama, Durbar, Clark Hotel—and other businesses were making lots of money because when the night clubs in Hollywood would close, the white people would come to Central Avenue for after-hour entertainment. It was rumored that policemen started writing ticket citations on the white people's cars in order to discourage them from coming to the flourishing Black night clubs. This ticket citation hurt the economy for Central Avenue's entertainment spot. This was a prominent Black neighborhood.

During the day the musicians would come to Ross Snider Playground to rehearse. We were able to watch and enjoy them since we were too young to go to the clubs.

I started to work at the Owl Drug Store on Vernon and Central Avenue, washing dishes in the cafeteria section. We were able to eat ice cream and as much food as we wanted. We had a ball! Then I went to work at the Old Ralph's Bakery on Washington and Seventh Avenue, washing pots and pans. The bakers would let us eat pastries when they took them out of the ovens. After a few days we were sick of pastries. The bakers laughed at us. They knew that they would not have any more eating from us. It took me several years before I could eat any pastries.

Later I started working as a waiter on the Southern Pacific Railroad on the diners. Troops were being transported to various camps.

In 1942, I started working for Douglas Aircraft in Santa Monica, along with several teenage Whites—we were assigned to the Paint Department. Our Foreman was a racist from St. Louis, Missouri. Our Lead man was a Black man who had been working there for six months. After a week I came to work and noticed that all the teen Whites that came to work the same time that I did were missing. So I asked our

Lead man where they were. He told me that all of them had been transferred to another department, which was a pay increase.

While we were discussing this injustice the Foreman came over and asked me why was I standing around talking instead of working. I told him I was trying to find out why all the Whites had been transferred to another department, with a pay raise. He said that they had previous experience. I told him that was not true because all of them had just finished high school and this was their first job. He then told me that if I did not like the way things were done here I could talk to the Supervisor.

I guess he thought that I would be afraid to talk to the Supervisor. Instead I told him to take me to the Supervisor. So he took me into the Supervisor's office. The Supervisor asked him what was wrong. The Foreman told him that I was complaining about how things were done here. Then the Supervisor asked me what things. I told him that I wanted to know why all the Whites that came in the same time that I did were transferred to another department with a pay increase, and none of us Blacks were. The Supervisor then asked the Foreman if this was true. The Foreman replied that he thought this was the way he wanted him to do things.

The Supervisor was very angry. He told the Foreman that when a name came to him with the Foreman's signature on it, he would O.K. transferring. He then told the Foreman that he wanted this policy stopped at once.

As a result of my making them aware of such injustice, all of us, including the Black Lead man who was afraid to complain, we were all transferred and given a raise. (Justice!)

DIFFERENT POT, BUT SAME SOUP

As I continued to live in Los Angeles I was shocked to discover that the injustices that we thought we had left in Texas were all right here. I also found out that the native-born Blacks, whose parents had been brought to Los Angeles as servants of Whites, were afraid to challenge any injustices. It took us Southerners to challenge and resolve some of the injustices. They were always telling us not to go in certain areas; my mother ignored them and went anyway. My mother was never a servant.

Chapter 1
MY ARMY EXPERIENCE IN 1943

MY ARMY EXPERIENCE IN 1943

I was drafted into the Army. I reported to Fort MacArthur and then was sent to Camp Stoneman in Pittsburg, California, where they started to separate the Whites from the Blacks.

The group that I was with was sent to Camp Swift in Texas. We were assigned to the 942nd Air Base Security Company B. When we were ordered to fall out, we found out that all of our officers for our Company were Black.

Our Company Commander was Captain Roach and the lieutenants were Lt. Johnson and Lt. Griffin. We were welcomed by Captain Roach. He told us that we would be working very hard, and they were going to make good soldiers out of us. We also found out that the other companies of Blacks all had white officers. After we had been there awhile with our officers, we saw how very educated and well trained they were. In those days they had to be smarter than Whites to justify their ranks. We started to really respect our officers and later we were always number one on inspections.

After we completed our basic training we were all given weekend passes. Outside Camp there were buses to take us to a small town near Bastrop. So we got on to the bus and sat down in the empty seats up front. Then the bus driver yelled at us and said, "You boys are in the wrong seats," and told us to go to the back of the bus. So we just sat there and did not move. Then the bus driver got off the bus and brought back a White MP from New York. He told the MP to make us move to the rear of the bus. The MP would not do it. So we rode up front into Bastrop and also rode up front on returning. Remember, this was in 1943.

The next day there was a bulletin ordering us to obey the Texas laws. William Mukes from Cincinnati, Ohio, and I had become very good friends so we asked the whole Company to hitchhike to Bastrop rather than ride in the rear of buses, so they agreed because Bastrop was close by.

I was then sent to Fort Sill, Oklahoma, to a cook and baker school. After arriving there the Major Sargent Ralph Carey asked me if my mother's name was Ruby Andrew. I told him, "yes." He then told me that he was married to my mother's half-sister, Pearl. That made him my uncle. Boy, what a thrill! He also told me that my mother's step-mother and her half-sister, Opal, lived nearby and gave me a weekend pass. He took me to see them in a military vehicle. My ego enlarged! Me, being driven by a Master Sargent. I had a super time while visiting.

After passing the classes, I was promoted to Technician Fifth Grade and sent back to Camp Swift. William Mukes had been promoted to Buck Sergeant. We still remained good friends.

After we completed our combat training, Captain Roach advised us that we would be shipping out tomorrow for overseas duties. He also told us that normally we would be restricted to the area, but since we had been such loyal and super soldiers he was issuing the entire company passes, and he knew that none of us would be AWOL tomorrow morning.

So we took vehicles and went to Bastrop to celebrate with the young ladies that we had met while we were stationed there. We were in the Club having a good time, when these Southern-type MP's started to take out their clubs to use on us. We felt that there was nothing to justify such an injustice; we used the folding chairs that we were sitting on as a defense. The MP's saw that they were out- numbered, so they left. We also left right away. We went back to Camp and the next morning early we were on our way overseas.

Chapter 2
OVERSEAS EXPERIENCE

OVERSEAS EXPERIENCE

We spent several days and nights on very rough waters. We were all very seasick. We finally docked on a Hawaiian island. What a relief to be on solid ground! We were then stationed on Sand Island. After we had gotten everything in order, we were given weekend passes to Honolulu. We started making the clubs. The young natives were very friendly and nice. They were either trying to sing like Nat King Cole or dance like Blacks. They preferred dancing with Blacks over Whites. This was before the Island became a state. They were very proud of their mixed races.

As we continued to party, we were invited to a Easter dance and told the admission was sixty-five cents. So we went back to camp all excited and waiting for Easter. We all got passes and went to the dance. We went to the window to pay to go in. Then we were told that they could not let us in. We thought the dance was off–limits to military troops. But, as we started to leave, we saw the White service men entering. So we went back and asked, "Why were they admitting Whites in and not allowing Blacks in?" That is when we were told that they had been given a direct order not to allow Blacks in. And since they were under Martial Law, they had to obey.

We were very disappointed and angry. Here we are, American soldiers, waiting to go into combat to defend the country and being treated like this! So we decided that we were not going to leave until we were allowed in the dance. So all at once the Jeeps came up and the Sergeant got out and started telling us to leave. We told that Sergeant that we were not leaving until we were allowed in the dance. Then another Jeep came up with a Lieutenant and a Provost Marshall. The Lieutenant asked the Sergeant why hadn't he carried out the order. The Sergeant told the Lieutenant, "Sir, if you want this order carried out you will have to carry it out yourself." Then Captain Roach came up and told us that the General who was from South Carolina had canceled all of our passes, and we were Absent Without Leave.

He told us to go back to our barracks. He promised that he would get this injustice resolved, even if he had to go all the way to Washington, D.C. We went back to our barracks and the next day the injustice was resolved. We continued going to Honolulu without any more problems (Justice!).

Later we were ordered to fall out and a Major told us that all of our officers were being promoted. That was the good news. Then we were told that the Black officers were being transferred because we were going into combat. All of the Black officers who had worked so hard training and preparing us for combat were denied getting the credit while we were in combat because they were Black. What an injustice!

We were than dismissed and told to go back to our barracks and prepare for shipment. We went into our barracks very sad and angry. Sergeant Mukes and I told the whole company that, since our Black officers were being denied credit in the combat area, we wanted the whole company to refuse to fall out. We were later ordered to fall out and no one did. Then we were given a direct order to fall out. Still no one fell out. Then we were told that we were being charged with mutiny. Still nobody responded. Finally a group of MP's came in and took all of us to the stockade. We were tried and convicted of mutiny. William Mukes and I were charged with being the instigators, and we were sentenced to die.

Chapter 3
SENTENCED TO DIE

SENTENCED TO DIE

The others were given life sentences. We were put on the rock piles and worked very hard. Later, by an act of God, Tokyo Rose, the propagandist, started to make this her main topic. She said America, which is supposed to be the home of the brave and the land of the free with liberty and justice for all, was guilty of racism. She continued talking about this on the radio and it became national news. Later William Mukes and I were told that our death sentences were reduced to life. Boy, what a relief to be off death row! We were still in prison when the war ended. We were later sent for rehabilitation. After rehabilitation we were assigned to the 132nd engineers.

I was then chosen to help make preparations for a Black soldier to be shot. He had accidentally killed a native woman. We were ordered to stay in our barracks until after he was shot. Waiting was rough. Then, when the shots were fired, it's hard to explain how we felt.

Then I was chosen to be the only Black guard to guard Japanese prisoners of war. We were briefed on the pros and cons and the do's and don'ts. We were also told that we would have five prisoners. Each group would have a prisoner that spoke English. We were to talk only to him to let him know what duties were on the agenda for each day. I obeyed the orders. However there was one White guard that ignored all orders; instead of talking with the prisoners that spoke English, he went to one of the prisoners and started ordering him to pick up a rock.

When the prisoner did nothing, he then would take the butt end of the rifle and start using it on the prisoner, while pointing to the rock shouting "Pick it up!" I guess after a while the prisoner would assume that he was talking about the rock and would nervously pick it up. Then the guard would say, "I knew you could speak English." Then I told the guard that was wrong and I asked him, "How would he feel if he was their prisoner!" His response was that they bombed Pearl Harbor and should be treated this way.

The next day when we went to pick up our prisoners, when the White guard came up, he was booed. And when I came up they cheered. Later, when my prisoners were given their breaks, they used the time to hand–carve things for me. I had the tokens mailed in 1946. I never received them. My prisoners were so dedicated to me.

One day I was nodding off, and they saw the Officer-of the-Day coming, and one of my prisoners woke me up. If he had not awakened me I would have been Court Martialed. Conditions got so bad between the White guards and the prisoners that there was a saying among them, "If you blink, you will stink!" meaning that they would be killed.

Chapter 4
HONORABLE DISCHARGE

HONORABLE DISCHARGE

I believe that we, as a Company rebelling, caused the Korean troops to be integrated. I also got my rank back and was given an Honorable Discharge.

I came home and found out that my parents had bought a home on Mariposa and Twelfth Street, and had bought a cleaning business on Melrose and Western. This was a predominately Jewish community. Both my parents worked in the business. They did very well; they had no problems. Their customers loved them and the service that they provided. One Jewish man would always come to the cleaners to just sit and chat with my father. When my parents decided to sell the cleaners, this Jewish man purchased the business. The new owner asked my father to consider becoming a partner with him, because the customers ceased coming after they discovered that my father no longer owned the business.

The new owner asked my father if he would just come and sit sometimes, so that the people would think that he still had a hand in the business. My father refused. He was a man of integrity.

Chapter 5
WHAT GOING TO CHURCH GOT ME!

WHAT GOING TO
CHURCH GOT ME!

I started going back to my church, Pilgrim Baptist on Forty-fifth and Wadsworth. One Sunday morning Paul Moore and I were standing in front of the church when Veraneace Lomack came by. She was on her way to visit a friend. She told us that she was on vacation from playing the organ for the church, from playing the piano for the Gospel Choir, and from directing the Youth Choir. That's when I was formally introduced to her. I knew of her before I went into the service, but she was only fourteen then. She had developed into a beautiful young lady. She then asked me to join the Youth Choir. So I did.

Later in 1946, we started to date. We dated until 1948 when we became engaged. On August 29, we became as one and went to San Diego for a weeks' honeymoon. I was working then for the Post Office as a Postman and also at the Terminal Annex.

LIFE WITH MY FAMILY

We have a son, Gerald, and two daughters, Sheila and Lisa. As my son got older I became his Scout Master and his Manager in Little League Baseball. Vera and I spent lots of time with the children. We always took them on vacations with us and when we were having parties with friends.

From our three children we have seven grand-children and eight great grand-children, and we love them all.

Chapter 6
FIGHTING FOR JUSTICE IN THE WORK PLACE

FIGHTING FOR JUSTICE
IN THE WORK PLACE

In 1949, the Golden State Milk Dairy hired me as a milkman. The Golden State Dairy was the only milk company that was hiring Blacks. So after I was given a route, I immediately started to let the customers of Carnation and Adhor know that these companies were not hiring Blacks. As a result I was able to get some of the Blacks to switch. I told them to call in and discontinue service, and when they were asked why to tell them that until they started to hire Blacks as milkmen they would not support them. After more and more Blacks discontinued their services, they finally started hiring Black milkmen. (Justice!)

In 1956, I was hired by the Sun Crest Beverage Company as a drive salesman. They also were the only beverage company hiring Blacks. So I started to let the merchants know that the other companies, namely Coca Cola, Pepsi Cola, Seven Up and Nehi, were not hiring Blacks . . . such an injustice! The merchants were also very supportive. They started to cut back on their orders and increase my orders. They also let those companies know why they were cutting back on their orders. And after a period of time they started hiring Blacks as driver salesmen. (Justice!)

My General Manager was so pleased with my increase in sales, that he moved me to a predominantly White area. And after my sales continued to increase, he called me into his office and told me how pleased he was with me. Then he told me that the areas of Encino, West Covino and Covino were putting in new shopping centers with chain store super-markets. He wanted to put me in these areas. He also stated that I would probably have some problems with some of the managers or receiving clerks. So if I did have any problems he wanted me to call him immediately. So I started to call on these chain stores as a driver salesman.

To my surprise things were working out well—after they saw that I was qualified and knew what I was doing. I did, however, come upon a racist who told me that he did not want to do business with me. I called my General Manager and told him. He then told me to put the person on the phone. After the racist explained that he wanted another driver salesman, my General Manager told him that our beverages had been authorized by his main office, and no one else would call on him. So he had me only after this. I had no more problems. (Justice!)

I continued working this area until I received a call from an old friend of mine, Brad Garrett. Brad and I had worked on previous jobs together. He was being made a distributor for the Hamms Beer—the first Black distributor. He had been working for H. W. Pingree Company as a salesman. The Pingree Company was a distributor of Millers, Hamms and Rainier Ale. Brad had recommended me to replace him. He explained that my job would be pre-selling the products. I would not have to deliver them. Also I would be making much more money. This was too much for me to turn down. So I went into the General Manager's office to let him know that I was leaving and giving him notice. He was not angry. He said he expected something was in the making when these calls came in asking for me. Instead of being angry, he wished me the best of everything. He also told me that if things did not work out I could come back with him.

I started working for H. W. Pingree Company in 1961. Brad Garrett took me into his area on the east side of Los Angeles. Afterward I found out that several of these merchants had been my customers when I was working for

Suncrest. This made the transition easier. I tried to always treat all my customers with respect, whether they were large or small, and to treat all races the same. That helped me toward making many friends.

Then the Hamms Brewery started using the bear in their commercials, and started an incentive program based on the greatest sales increase over the previous year. My route had the greatest number of new accounts and the most case increases sold. As a result I ended up with enough redeemable coupons to do the Christmas shopping for my entire family. The owners were pleased with me. They had proven to me that they were only concerned about getting returns on their investments. No matter what race you were. (Justice!)

Later the company merged with their Compton disributor, and we were extended to Orange County. I was given a different area. Then the Sick Rainer Brewery decided to start brewing Spur Malt Liquor to be competitive with Old English 800. I was sent up to the brewery for a meeting with the brewery staff. I had no pre-knowledge of what the meeting was about until I was brought into a room where there was a large group around a table. Then I discovered that I was the main attraction. They were planning to do lots of commercials on the radio advertising Spur Malt Liquor. They wanted me to decide which person I thought would be better to do the commercials, Moms Maberly or Lou Rawls. This was before Lou Rawls had made an appearance on The Ed Sullivan Show. So I told them that I would choose Lou Rawls because he was much younger than Moms Maberly. So they took my advice and used Lou Rawls.

A few weeks later Spud Malt Liquor started to sell. Then Lou Rawls made an appearance on The Ed Sullivan Show. The sales of Spur Malt Liquor skyrocketed. The small brewery could hardly supply the market. They were very happy with my choice. After a while it was time to renew Lou Rawls' contract. The agent wanted more money than the small Sick Rainer Brewery could afford. I don't know if Lou Rawls ever knew that I was the one who recommended him.

Phillip Morris Tobacco Company purchased the Miller Brewing Company, and I was sent to Chicago for a convention. I was chosen over all the older workers because of my better performance. (Justice!) The owner and I were representing our company. After arriving in Chicago we were informed that they were coming out with a Miller Lite Beer and told how many billions of dollars they were going to spend toward the advertising. When I heard them talking about billions of dollars I couldn't believe my ears.

They were also going to have some incentive programs and would be spending lots of money. I was very glad to hear that. So after the convention we came back to Los Angeles and I started immediately working to make more money. My customers were very supportive, and as a result I came in among the top salesmen with new accounts and with the most cases sold. I received a very big commission check. The owner was very proud and I was promoted to Marketing Director. My territory was from east to Orange County and west to Manhattan Beach (Justice!).

Then the Koreans from Seoul, Korea, started to purchase liquor stores and small markets. They had lots of money to work with, but their knowledge of this marketing area was limited. So when I would call on some of the accounts, I could see where they were in violation. I would take the time and call these violations to their attention, including violations of the Fair Trade Law. They would thank me for being so nice to them.

They would also call other friends of theirs and tell them about me. This mushroomed into quite a task because when I went into their stores they wanted me to see if they were in violation. It was lots of work, but it paid off later. They trusted me and were trying to give me as much business as possible. Then a money order company that most of the Koreans were using went bankrupt, and all their money orders were coming back unpaid. Our Credit Manager had been trying to collect for them.

The Koreans were refusing to make the money orders good because they had been advised to wait until they had gotten their money. So the Credit Manager asked me if I would see if I could collect. So I was given a bunch of money orders, and when I went to collect on the accounts I was told the same thing that they had told the Credit Manager. I took the time to explain to them that we could not legally let them charge until the money orders were made good because they were for charges that were over forty-two days. They would have to either make the money orders good or pay cash on all of their deliveries. Because of the trust they had in me they gave me cash for the money orders. When I came back the Credit Manager was shocked. She started calling me "Sam Spade."

I was later sent back to Chicago to represent the company at a seminar. We were told that Miller Lite was selling like mad, and they were very pleased. We were taken through the brewery and shown everything about the brewing of Millers'. It was a learning experience. We were all tested on our sales abilities. I passed along with others, and they congratulated us and sent us back to California and other states.

Then the brewery sent out some representatives. They requested only me to take them throughout the industry to show them the best locations for billboards to post their signs. I was thrilled and honored to be chosen over all the other personnel because of my track record (Justice!).

Chapter 7
RETIRED AND STILL FIGHTING

RETIRED AND STILL FIGHTING

After thirty-five years of working with the public I decided it was about time for me to retire. So when I gave the owners my notice they were very sad to hear it. They tried to talk me out of retiring. The owner wanted me to continue being available and to assist as a supervisor. I said, "Sorry, but I could not do it."

About two weeks after retiring, I received a call from the owner telling me that some of the Korean merchants were refusing to give anybody the checks that were due until I came by. So when I went into the accounts, I was welcomed with open arms. Immediately they started handing me checks. I explained that I had retired, and in the future please give them the checks. All of this was because they trusted me.

I took the checks in and, boy, was my ex-boss happy. I was given a going-away party, and they had money and many gifts for me. It was a happy and sad occasion.

I rested awhile and then I really started to work very closely with the Police Department. My wife, Vera, was elected as Block Captain and I worked with her. She later decided that she was going to resign as Block Captain. That's when I was elected as Block Captain. We built the Block up with all of the neighbors. Also, other areas heard about how well we were doing. They asked to join our Block Club. We took them in.

As I continued to work very closely with the Police Department, I saw that there were injustices toward Blacks. The well-qualified Blacks were being passed over for senior lead officers. After watching and talking with all of the officers, I was thoroughly convinced that injustices existed. So I went to the Sergeant and told her what I had observed. She wanted to deny it. So I went to the Captain, but nothing was done about it. Then I spoke with the Deputy Chief, who knew me quite well. And I told him that same thing that I had discussed with the others. I also told him that the Blacks were very qualified and were working hard toward curbing crime. They also had established a good rapport in the communities. After we had discussed the injustices, he asked me for the name of the most qualified. I gave it to him and he wrote it in his book. A few days later the Black officer was made a Senior Lead Officer. (Justice!)

Then I read in the paper that the Black Captain at the Station had been given an ultimatum, to either resign or be terminated because he had been charged with shoving a White civilian woman that worked in his office. So we as Block Captains decided to look into the matter.

We found out that the Captain saw this white woman with all these things on her desk, and the Captain had asked her about them. She told the Captain that this was personal business. The Captain then told her that she was not supposed to be taking care of personal business on company time. That's when she claimed the Captain then shoved her. Her word was being taken over the Captain's. (Injustice!) The woman had lied.

Then I drafted a letter stating that after thoroughly checking, we, as a community, felt that a grave injustice was being dealt to this Captain. I told them that the Captain was only doing his job, by not allowing personal business on the clock. I sent copies to the Chief of Police, the Mayor, and the Commissioners.

A week later I received a letter from the Chief of Police thanking me for taking the time to look into this issue, and that the Captain would have a fair hearing. The Captain was not terminated. He was transferred downtown at the same rank. (Justice!)

However, I have not received a call or a letter from the Black Captain thanking me.

In 1992 when the riots began, the Chief of Police was out of town. I read in the paper that when he returned he had said he was going to demote officers from the Assisting Chief down. One night about 9:00 p.m., I received a call from the Black Captain of a Station. He said he was very upset about what was happening, and he wanted to hear a friendly voice. I told him not to worry, and that we would look into the matter.

I then drafted another letter and sent copies to the Chief of Police, the Mayor, and the Commissioners stating that I know how the system works. There is a chain of command so let's stop blaming others and get these problems resolved. No one was demoted!

The Black Captain is now a Police Chief up north. The Police Department gave him a going-away celebration to which I was invited. The Department was so pleased with the letter that I had sent in that they asked my permission to read the letter at the well-attended celebration. It was read and all of the officers applauded me. (Justice!)

I was asked to work on the Oral Board to help select the most qualified officers. I was the only civilian and the only Black. (Justice!)

After the riots the Korean merchants invited me to meet with them in Korea Town. They were concerned with problems they were having as merchants. I was the Guest Speaker. As I addressed the merchants I told them that they had to make adjustments first. This is America and, as merchants, you are paid to render a decent service to all your customers, whether in Beverly Hills or South Central Los Angeles, and all the Blacks are not thieves. Don't just take money out of the communities, but put some back into it.

Then a supermarket located at Slauson and Crenshaw dismissed a Black manager and had planned to replace him with a White manager. I was in the store when the District Manager came in. I asked him why were they putting a White manager in this predominantly Black area instead of putting a Black. His reply was that they could not find a Black. I told him that they were not looking hard enough. I also told him that as long as they were not putting Blacks in predominantly

White areas that we would not let them put a White manager here. They found a Black manager in a hurry. (Justice!)

Then a Thrifty Drug Store in the Slauson and Crenshaw area hired a Black woman manager. The store was very run-down, dirty, and not stocked with all products. As a result, customers had stopped shopping there. As soon as this Black woman manager took over the store, she gave it a thorough cleaning—with a very limited crew. So she was having to work very hard herself. After the store was cleaned up and had all products available, the customers started to come back. What a transition!

I was so impressed that I took the Senator from this District, and we inspected the entire store. She was also pleased. After the business picked-up, she asked for more help—which the District Manager refused to allow. So I made an arrangement to meet at the store with the District Manager. We met and I told him that this manager had worked very hard toward cleaning the store up and getting back customers, and she needs help, and we are not going to let her be worked to death. A few days later she was given help. (Justice!)

The street that I live on had all kinds of potholes, cracks and other bad conditions. We were told that a shortage of manpower was why nothing was being done. But they had worked on the streets west of Crenshaw twice in four years. And they still were not working on my street. So I got on the phone and called in complaining again. I then asked them if Crenshaw Boulevard was the "Mason and Dixon Line." After that call, the Commissioner called and told me that a Supervisor would be out in a day or so and my street would be repaired, and it was. (Justice!)

Later a Black assistant Police Chief had been sent to Germany on police business, and after he returned he was not told that he had been demoted. He found it out while watching television with his wife as they were dining out. So we C.P.A.B. members—Al Williams, Catherine and myself, along with many others—decided to go to City Hall and protest this injustice. It worked because the victim is now our Chief of Police and is doing a good job.

Currently I am a member of the Community Police Advisory Board, Councilperson Ruth Galanter's Advisory Board, and the Kenneth Hahn Parks and Recreation Advisory Board. I work very closely with Mr. Hawkins at the Whitney Young Continuation School.

I am a member of Morningside United Church of Christ. My Pastor is the Reverend Mark Rohrbaugh.

My objective is to be a part of the solution rather than a

part of the problem. Help make America a country that is truly liberty and justice for all. Amen.

My mother's ancestors were here long before Columbus and the Mayflower arrived. So we are really Americans. We were never taught that we were inferior to anybody, but God. My mother lived to witness 102 years.

In conclusion I want to thank God. Vera and I were happily married for nearly 53 years, we had a beautiful life together, and a wonderful family. She made her transition on July 29, 2001. Vera's spirit will forever encompass my soul. And we are still courting Amen!

To you, the reader, may this book encourage you to stand up for justice for all—regardless of race, creed, or color. Then, and only then, will the human race live out its creed of harmony and peace forever?

Family and Employment
Pictures and Certificates

Hubert Andrew with his mother Ruby Andrew

Hubert with his darling wife Vera

Hubert Andrew and his granddaughter Tanya Maxwell
Tanya is receiving her B.A. Degree from Calif. State L. A.

Hubert, Lisa, Vera, Shelia and Gerald

Hubert cousins Mary Moore, Karen Moore and
Deputy Police Chief Maurice Moore

Five generations
Hubert Andrew, Lisa Abernathy, Tanya Maxwell,
(Baby) Raven, Desmond and Ruby Andrew

Hubert and Veraneace Andrew Wedding
Father and Mother:
Bristol Andrew and Ruby Andrew
Groom and Bride:
Hubert and Veraneace Andrew
Father-in-law and Mother-in-law:
Lemuel Lomack and Bessie Lomack

Hubert brothers and sisters:
Chester, Bristol, Robert, Roy, Chauncey and Russell

Hubert Cousins:
Karen Moore, Mary Moore and
Deputy Police Chief Maurice Moore

Graduating class of Miller High Lite Marketing Director School

Certificate of Completion
Awarded to Hebert Andrew
Sales Supervisor Training Seminar

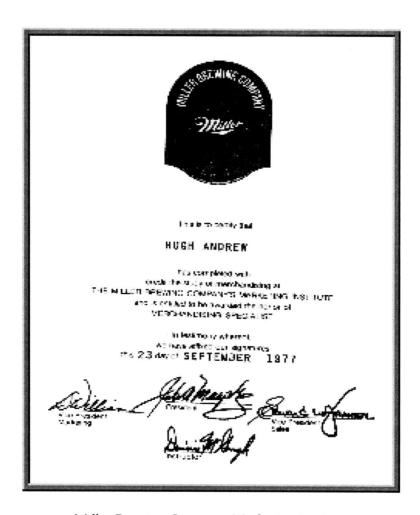

Miller Brewing Company Marketing Institute
Certificate of Completion
Awarded to Hebert Andrew as
Merchandising Specialist

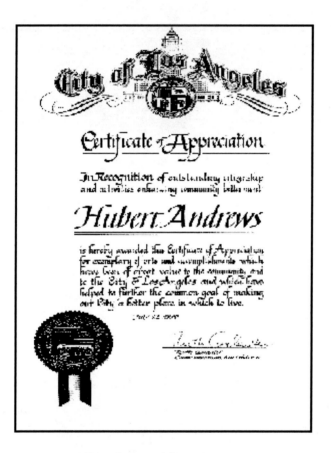

Certificate of Appreciation
Awarded to Hubert Andrew
By the City of Los Angeles